#SUCCESSFUL CORPORATE LEARNING
tweet Book10

Making Training Stick—Transforming Knowledge

into Performance

By John Moxley, PhD, and Mitchell Levy

Foreword by Ken Lewis

An Actionable Business Journal

E-mail: info@thinkaha.com
20660 Stevens Creek Blvd., Suite 210
Cupertino, CA 95014

Published by THiNKaha®
20660 Stevens Creek Blvd., Suite 210, Cupertino, CA 95014
http://thinkaha.com

First Printing: October 2013
Paperback ISBN: 978-1-61699-112-8 (1-61699-112-7)
eBook ISBN: 978-1-61699-113-5 (1-61699-113-5)
Place of Publication: Silicon Valley, California, USA
Paperback Library of Congress Number: 2012954461

Trademarks

Warning and Disclaimer

Advance Praise

"Pithy, practical, and profound. Moxley and Levy have written a book of tweetable proverbs for achieving learning and performance nirvana. This book is packed with ideas that you can use right away."

Marty Rosenheck, PhD, Chief Learning Strategist, Cognitive Advisors

"Major kudos for capturing concisely what good learning looks like and the myriad factors that must work together to make it so. All the right things to do before, during, and immediately after the learning."

Art Paton, Manager, Learning and Development, Baxter Healthcare

"140 tips and best practices from two of the top professionals in the field of learning. A great fit for today's workplace!"

Joe DiDonato, Editor-at-Large, *Elearning! Magazine*

"I think this book would be incredibly helpful for anyone that needs a primer on corporate training and making learning stick. These are things that one can easily implement."

Michael Sabbag, VP of People and Culture, BGT Partners

Nothing gets done until you believe you can do it.
With great love to my mother, Virginia, and my wife, Constance,
the two most supportive individuals I have ever known.

Acknowledgments

Writing a book, even a simple one like this, was more challenging than I expected (especially in trying to distill a body of ideas into the simple statements that comprise the THiNKaha® format). Mitchell Levy provided the initial encouragement and structure around which we wrapped these ideas. Diane Vo, my editor, showed tremendous patience, coupled with an insightful eye and the gentle prodding I needed throughout. Many of the ideas in this book come from the work of BJ Fogg, Daniel Pink, Chip and Dan Heath, and Charles Duhigg, who have written extensively on positive psychology, intrinsic motivation, and what it takes to get people to adopt new behaviors and turn them into habits. Many others contributed ideas as well, including Marty Rosenheck, David Orr, Mark Steiner, Art Paton, and Susan Gervasi. My gratitude to them and the others too numerous to mention.

Why We Wrote This Book

Today's training industry is capable of creating great course experiences, whether in the classroom or online. Over the years I have observed too many cases in which that particular investment was wasted because the behavior change never occurs. In spite of our best intentions, new habits never form, the work environment conflicts with the training objectives, and lasting change never happens. The sad thing is that while the remedy is often simple, it rarely occurs. It's like running 26 miles, thinking we are done, and never going the last 0.2 miles to finish the marathon.

And we do that over and over and over.

So, Mitchell and I decided to focus on that last 0.2 miles, the hardest part of the race. What does it really take to transform knowledge into new behaviors and make training stick? What does it take to create lasting results? To me, those lasting improvements are the meaningful legacy we (learning professionals) leave behind, not what went on in the course. We are not in the entertainment business, we are not in the knowledge business, we are in the change business. It is only by that standard that we should ask the question, "Did I make a difference?" We hope the simple ideas in this book help you make a lasting impact on the organizations you serve, and make training stick!

John Moxley, PhD

How to Read a THiNKaha® Book
A Note from the Publisher

The THiNKaha series is the CliffsNotes of the 21st century. The value of these books is that they are contextual in nature. Although the actual words won't change, their meaning will change every time you read one as your context will change. Experience your own "aha!" moments ("ahas") with a THiNKaha book; ahas are looked at as "actionable" moments—think of a specific project you're working on, an event, a sales deal, a personal issue, etc. and see how the ahas in this book can inspire your own ahas, something that you can specifically act on. Here's how to read one of these books and have it work for you.

1. Read a THiNKaha book (these slim and handy books should only take about 15–20 minutes of your time!) and write down one to three actionable items you thought of while reading it. Each journal-style THiNKaha book is equipped with space for you to write down your notes and thoughts underneath each aha.

2. Mark your calendar to re-read this book again in 30 days.

3. Repeat step #1 and write down one to three more ahas that grab you this time. I guarantee that they will be different than the first time. BTW: this is also a great time to reflect on the actions taken from the last set of ahas you wrote down.

After reading a THiNKaha book, writing down your ahas, re-reading it, and writing down more ahas, you'll begin to see how these books contextually apply to you. THiNKaha books advocate for continuous, lifelong learning. They will help you transform your ahas into actionable items with tangible results until you no longer have to say "aha!" to these moments—they'll become part of your daily practice as you continue to grow and learn.

As Thought Leader Architect & CEO of THiNKaha, I definitely practice what I preach. I read *#POSITIVITY at WORK tweet*, *#MANAGING YOUR VIRTUAL BOSS tweet*, and one new book once a month and take away two to three different action items from each of them every time. Please e-mail me your ahas today!

Mitchell Levy
publisher@thinkaha.com

Contents

How to Use This Book

In reading this book, many of you will gain five to 10 insights that you can easily and immediately apply, in part because these will be reminders of what you already know. In other cases an idea provokes some thought, but because of the concise format of the book we did not have room to elaborate with a story or example that provides the context that makes the idea crystal clear.

If you find yourself in that spot, ask yourself how you might use the concept in your work—you provide the example. If you allow yourself a few minutes to ponder how you could apply some of these ideas, or just put the book aside for a few days and return back to it, you will be rewarded with a new perspective that will help you creatively apply these concepts—it's all in the application!

John Moxley, PhD

moxl@msn.com

www.linkedin.com/in/johnpmoxley

Foreword by Ken Lewis

When I encountered this deceptively slim book I was a little bewildered at first blush. The format incorporates many tips I have come to depend on over the years. But after I set it aside and returned back to it, it became clear that something different was going on. For me, the book began to take on the character of a collection of Zen haiku. It wasn't just the concise nature of the "ahas," it was the sense that much was intentionally being left unsaid—where, I wondered, were the examples? Where is the context that makes these kinds of tips immediately accessible? In contrast to many business books that are short on ideas and long on anecdotes, this is the exact opposite.

True, many of the pointers for making learning stick can be put to immediate use—the kind of simple tricks of the trade I've come to expect. In that sense this book is useful for the novice looking for practical techniques and quick results. It is also a powerful tool for the experienced learning professional who needs a deeper framework for driving lasting behavioral change. The simple yet powerful ideas are rooted in proven techniques of motivation, change management, memory retention, and habit formation. Applied creatively, your effort will be more than amply rewarded, and your learners will advance from temporary knowledge retention to lasting behavioral improvement that drives personal fulfillment and tangible business impact.

Ken Lewis
Creative Director and Teambuilding Facilitator
Motivation Media Inc.

Section 1

Training Nirvana

In the past, training organizations were held accountable for learning by measuring classroom numbers (e.g., attendees, tests), learner satisfaction, and knowledge assessments. Today, we are accountable for organizational results—the application of knowledge and skills to accomplish business objectives. To achieve those results we strive to create a variety of learning experiences that are engaging and impactful. But what exactly is the ideal experience we are trying to provide?

We call that ideal experience *training nirvana*, where learners assess their capabilities, develop their skills, adapt their behaviors, and build lasting habits to achieve personal goals and meet organizational needs. In this section, we define different aspects of a training nirvana, and provide tips on how to successfully focus learning in your organization.

1

In training nirvana, individuals are not coerced into learning. Instead, they apply what they have learned willingly and eagerly.

_____

_____

_____

2

Learners understand what is expected, believe it is good for them, and believe that they can do it.

_____

_____

_____

3

Everyone wants microwave training.[1]
Reach nirvana by providing training that
is quick, timely, painless, and relevant to
learners' jobs.

_____

_____

_____

1. Quick and easy training (compared to conventional training that
takes time to prepare/"heat up"). If you don't do it right, you may get
burned.

4

In training nirvana, learners focus on what they need to do to get the job done, learn it, and immediately apply it.

_____

_____

_____

5

Training is simple, concrete, practical, relevant, and provides opportunities to practice, recognizing accomplishments large and small.

_____

_____

_____

6

In training nirvana, learners look forward to using what they have learned right away (and are expected to).

_____

_____

_____

7

Provide ongoing learning opportunities, time for reinforcement, and other knowledge transfer activities.

_____

_____

_____

8

Create an environment where learners can apply their new skills and techniques without political or cultural resistance.

_____

_____

_____

9

Learners focus on behaviors, receive feedback, are recognized for improvement, help others, and apply what they learn on the job.

_____

_____

_____

10

We have succeeded when learners become self-motivated, work autonomously, and actively pursue personal development.

_____

_____

_____

11

When learners are engaged, skilled, and focused on achieving the organization's objectives, we have accomplished our mission.

_____

_____

_____

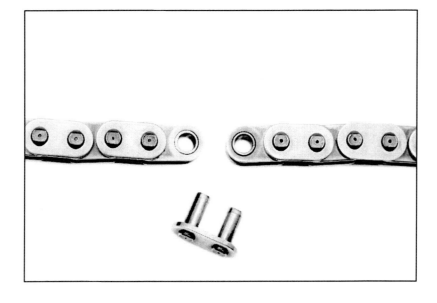

Section II

Why Traditional Training Fails Today

This section reviews the traditional assumptions and approaches to training, and why event-based approaches fail when they are not linked to behaviors and habits—especially in today's work environment.

12

Traditional training typically focuses
on what can be easily measured
(e.g., knowledge acquisition), and not
on application.

_____

_____

_____

13

Traditional training does not provide the means to trigger and track on-the-job applications of learning.

_____

_____

_____

14

Traditional training does not provide the feedback required to refine skills and replace old habits with new ones.

_____

_____

_____

15

Traditional skill practice lacks the variety and deep repetition needed to achieve outstanding performance.

_____

_____

_____

16

Our knowledge prevents us from seeing our learners' points of view. Our minds fill in blanks with info that learners may not know.

_____

_____

_____

17

Practice and feedback must occur often and be spread evenly over time to achieve long-term change.

_____

_____

_____

18

Imparting knowledge doesn't necessarily influence behavior. Only by influencing behavior will we see lasting change.

_____

_____

_____

19

Giving trainees concepts with few opportunities for practice leaves them unprepared for tasks that are beyond what they have practiced.

_____

_____

_____

20

Lasting behavior change requires a change of heart as well as a change of mind. Rapid changes of heart require transformational experiences.

_____

_____

_____

Section III

Bridging the Gap between Knowledge and Performance

This section presents a simple model for behavior change that goes beyond knowledge acquisition. We include principles of deep learning, motivation, and habit-building.

21

Lasting behavior change requires addressing four aspects of change: knowledge, attitude, skill, and habit.

_____

_____

_____

22

Before you design training, find its core idea. Make it simple and specific as it drives and reinforces everything you include.

_____

_____

_____

23

Ask yourself, "What is the one thing I want people to do or remember in six months?"

_____

_____

_____

24

Factor in Maslow's hierarchy of needs: physiological, safety, belonging and love, esteem, and self-actualization/self-transcendence.[2]

_____

_____

_____

2. Saul McLeod, "Maslow's Hierarchy of Needs," *Simply Psychology*, last modified 2012, http://www.simplypsychology.org/maslow.html.

25

Get a learner's attention by breaking a
pattern. Change the course structure,
format, how you promote learning, how
you reinforce it, etc.

_____

_____

_____

26

Identify emotional attachments to current
processes/ideas. Create a compelling case
for the need to learn new skills, behaviors
& processes.

_____

_____

_____

27

Dramatic improvement is fueled by a series of small changes that depend on passionate commitment, dogged repetition, and regular feedback.

_____

_____

_____

28

Without feedback, behavior will never change. Online learning provides knowledge feedback, but it rarely provides feedback on skills.

_____

_____

_____

29

Commit to consistent coaching and feedback to perfect new behaviors and turn them into regular habits.

30

Without mentors or coaches, learners must learn to self-assess, using tools that enable them to apply objective criteria.

31

Developing expertise requires deep and deliberate practice. Repetition matters!

_____

_____

_____

32

Expertise requires the direction, drive, feedback, and support of a great coach.

_____

_____

_____

33

Deep expertise requires passion—the drive to do deliberate repetitive practice. Great coaches ignite that passion.

_____

_____

_____

34

Post-training cohort discussion groups require strong leaders and meaningful goals to sustain focus and engagement.

_____

_____

_____

35

Remind learners to seek constant critical feedback, and encourage them to immediately apply the things they learn.

_____

_____

_____

36

Give "merit badges" for mastering a new skill, and advanced ones for teaching others.

_____

_____

_____

37

Choose practical (and immediately useful) skills.

_____

_____

_____

38

Reflective checklists allow learners to self-assess their performance. Alternatively, record and show feedback rather than give it verbally.

_____

_____

_____

39

Give your learners opportunities to practice, make mistakes, and get feedback (or they'll practice with your customers).

_____

_____

_____

40

Before moving to the next topic, do a practice activity for your learners to build a little proficiency and sense of accomplishment.

_____

_____

_____

41

Examples of follow-up activities to drive retention: forums, tips, examples, new scenarios, games, teaching others, sharing successes, etc.

_____

_____

_____

Section IV

Promoting Retention and Skill Development

This section explores techniques for improving knowledge retention through application, skill practice, and other means of activating the learning process to build proficiency. We look at web-based mobile and social learning techniques that can automate the reinforcement process, and are scaled to work in a fast-paced, time-constrained work environment.

42

Use Qstream (qstream.com) to send questions to mobile devices at set intervals as a means of testing and activating knowledge.

_____

_____

_____

43

Use Axonify (axonify.com) to automate the process of reinforcing learning at spaced intervals that are personalized to each learner's needs.

_____

_____

_____

44

Use simple, unexpected, emotional stories to illustrate key points. Be counterintuitive to make points memorable.

_____

_____

_____

45

Summarize key points in sound bites—compact communication with a punch is more memorable.

_____

_____

_____

46

People remember ideas that are simple, unexpected, concrete, credentialed, or carry emotional impact.

_____

_____

_____

47

Stories generate interest, curiosity & build emotional connections. Use the Velcro theory of memory: the more hooks to the story the better.

_____

_____

_____

48

Take a lesson from proverbs—they are simple and profound stories that illustrate rules of thumb for behavior.

_____

_____

_____

49

Analogies are a way to pack a lot of meaning into small messages using examples people can relate to.

_____

_____

_____

50

Give learners enough information to be useful, but a little at a time instead of all at once. Spread out learning so sessions are ≤ 90 min.

_____

_____

_____

51

Chunk your content into categories containing seven or fewer items to be more memorable.

52

Create a mnemonic phrase, story, or picture to improve retention of factual information.

53

Train in the context in which learners will use it. Environmental cues enhance recall (e.g., train sales reps in their stores).

_____

_____

_____

54

Maximize learner engagement by matching difficulty level to ability level. Allow a balance of challenge and satisfaction.

_____

_____

_____

55

Use progressively more difficult scenarios. Remove scaffolding (support) to increase difficulty, build confidence & mimic on-the-job stress.

_____

_____

_____

56

Introducing higher difficulty not only builds skills, but also helps learners see that setbacks are not permanent.

57

Progressively increase task difficulty by moving from observation to recognition to recall.

58

Design activities that allow your learners to practice in the same way that they eventually will need to perform.

_____

_____

_____

59

Provide job aids to simplify tasks from difficult "recall the steps" to easier "follow these steps," reducing the need to rely on memory.

_____

_____

_____

60

Repetition builds better retention if you vary the format (e.g., games/puzzles, debates, flashcards, etc.).

_____

_____

_____

61

A big part of why games are good at developing skills is the frequency and variety of feedback mechanisms.

_____

_____

_____

62

Sleep improves memory consolidation. Stretching training over days helps learners review, reflect, and consolidate their memories.

63

Nobody wants to bike straight uphill all the time. Give your learners chances to rest. Let them acclimate before advancing.

_____

_____

_____

64

When dealing with unsatisfying or difficult practice, take the focus off the activity. Connect it to the learner's values and self-discipline.

_____

_____

_____

65

To get learners' attention and drive effort, ask interesting questions, pose problems, and withhold information to trigger curiosity.

_____

_____

_____

66

When introducing a new topic, create a mystery that draws in learners. Provide the answer later, and connect the dots to the core idea.

_____

_____

_____

67

Let learners express opinions. Justifying their opinions results in further analysis and more associations to their other schemas.

_____

_____

_____

68

Instead of just telling learners the correct answers, provide feedback that shows the result or consequence of their choices.

_____

_____

_____

69

Use anecdotes. Stories with vivid images and concrete details are more understandable (and credible) than terse lectures.

_____

_____

_____

70

Learners need to know: "Will it be worth it?" "Can I do it?" "Why?" "Why now?"

_____

_____

_____

71

Don't try to put all knowledge into learners' heads; figure out how to put some of it into a tool.

_____

_____

_____

72

Learning may be serious, but the process
need not be solemn. Keep it fun
and learners will focus, work hard, and
retain more.

Section V

Enabling Behavioral Change

"Plant a tiny habit in [the] right spot, and it will grow [without] further coaxing."[3]

-BJ Fogg

This section explores tools and techniques that reinforce behavioral change and habit formation. We review examples of practice, apps, messaging, trigger systems, to-do lists, and related web technologies that can be leveraged to drive longer-term behavioral change.

---

3. BJ Fogg, Twitter post, March 31, 2011, 6:54 a.m., https://twitter.com/bjfogg/status/53455036784717824.

73

When people successfully form good habits, they get happy and are motivated to form more good habits. Build on small successes.

_____

_____

_____

74

Habits form quickly if the efforts are focused—send daily reminders so that learners respond each day to questions about progress.

_____

_____

_____

75

Start with what learners already do. Tie new habits to existing habits (anchors). Anchors act as vital triggers for new habits.

_____

_____

_____

76

Have learners practice, over and over. Start easy, and then move up to add challenge.

_____

_____

_____

77

Learners can measure progress by asking, "Am I proficient? An expert? Can I teach others?"

78

Have learners apply their new skills to their own needs. Start with small challenges for early successes, and let them direct themselves.

79

Diligent performers celebrate more than strugglers. Celebrate success every time— even if it is just saying, "Nice job!"

80

If you are not building the behavior you want, revise your approach. Try a different anchor, time of day, reward/celebration, etc.

81

Only three things change behavior in the long term:

1. An epiphany.
2. A change in context.
3. Taking baby steps.[4]

_____

_____

_____

---

4. BJ Fogg, PhD, "Tiny Habits," *Tiny Habits,* last modified February 23, 2013, http://tinyhabits.com.

82

Individuals change when they have a combination of capacity, incentive, and control. Training gets them on the path to capacity.

_____

_____

_____

83

Autonomy drives engagement. Allow learners to personalize their takeaways and action plans.

_____

_____

_____

84

Connect your learners. Ask them to share one thing they learned in their training with their team, or have them train someone else.

_____

_____

_____

85

Track progress. Have learners tally how many times they apply a skill, and plot a graph to measure accomplishment.

_____

_____

_____

86

Share post-training application activities for social comparison. Everyone likes recognition and being on the leaderboard.

87

Allow peers to observe each other's performances for feedback.

88

Focus on "goldilocks" tasks—neither too easy or too hard. Small enough to be achievable but large enough to be meaningful.

_____

_____

_____

89

If your direct report has attended a learning event, ask him or her, "Now what?" Make follow-up steps explicit.

_____

_____

_____

90

Practice and master one thing at a time. Do not encourage multitasking of new learning.

_____

_____

_____

91

Focus learners on what is most important and express the urgency to do it <u>now</u>.

_____

_____

_____

92

We are engaged in a war with distraction, so pick your battles carefully. Learners have limited attention, time, and energy.

_____

_____

_____

93

Instill your learners with a belief in change, and energize them with your passion. Feed their passion with recognition and support.

_____

_____

_____

94

Focus first on behaviors, not outcomes. Otherwise, learners may cheat to get to the outcomes.

_____

_____

_____

95

Vicarious online simulations can substitute for real experience. It can mean a well-told story or step-by-step scenario.

_____

_____

_____

96

Don't just *teach* learners how to do a
process. See if there's a way to streamline
the process to make it simpler and easier
to perform.

97

When addressing the performance
environment ask, "What else can we do
(besides training) that will allow learners
to succeed?"

98

Connect to intrinsic motivators. Give learners autonomy, connect cohorts, recognize accomplishment, and reinforce the higher purpose.

_____

_____

_____

99

When a respected individual attempts a vital behavior and succeeds, it motivates others more than almost any other influence.

_____

_____

_____

100

To break bad habits reinforced by learners' existing social networks, place them in new groups that reward the right behaviors.

_____

_____

_____

101

If using extrinsic rewards, ensure that they come soon (e.g., reward small improvements), are gratifying, and clearly tied to behaviors.

_____

_____

_____

102

Sometimes, it's easier to change the situation than the person. Instead of creating new behaviors, provide workflows with easy-to-use tools.

_____

_____

_____

103

Don't exhaust your learners with too many expectations and/or decisions. Perceived resistance may actually be exhaustion.

104

When you exhaust learners you limit their self-control, creativity, focus, and ability to persist in the face of frustration or failure.

105

Remember that if you reach your learners' minds, but not their hearts, they will have direction without motivation.

_____

_____

_____

106

Engage learners' emotional sides to get their attention, improve retention, and energize them to follow through.

_____

_____

_____

107

Lack of follow-through may be a lack of clarity. Give learners clear post-training direction. Uncertainty is an excuse to do nothing.

_____

_____

_____

108

Decision paralysis can be deadly for change because the most familiar path is always the status quo, and people prefer the familiar.

_____

_____

_____

109

Change requires translating ambiguous goals into concrete behaviors. In short, to make a change, you need to script the critical moves.

_____

_____

_____

110

The world doesn't always want what you want. You want to change how others are acting, but they get a vote.

111

The most basic way to make people care is to piggyback something they don't yet care about with something they do care about.

112

Appeal to self-interest; don't bury it or talk around it. Make it personal for learners: "You will be able to ..."

_____

_____

_____

113

Spell out the benefit of the benefit. People don't buy quarter-inch drill bits. They buy quarter-inch holes to hang their kid's pictures.

_____

_____

_____

114

In forming opinions people seem to ask not, "What's in it for me?" but rather, "What's in it for my group?"

_____

_____

_____

115

Three strategies to make people care: use associations to what they already care about, appeal to self-interest, and appeal to identity.

_____

_____

_____

116

Empathy as a motivator emerges from the *particular* rather than the *pattern*. A single compelling illustration beats a range of statistics.

_____

_____

_____

117

Stories illustrate causal relationships people hadn't recognized & highlight unexpected, resourceful ways to solve problems.

_____

_____

_____

118

A credible idea makes people believe. An emotional idea makes people care. The right stories make people act.

_____

_____

_____

119

Use social proof; cite people whose opinions you respect. If you tell learners something is useful, they're more likely to try it.

_____

_____

_____

120

Learners need to feel confident with new challenges or skills. They have to believe they can do it before they commit.

_____

_____

_____

121

Change is a process, not an event. Any time you want learners to change their behavior, it's a process, and it needs to be reinforced.

122

For people to change, you must provide crystal-clear direction: clear intent, and clear behaviors. Vague direction leads to decision paralysis.

123

Direct the Rider, motivate the Elephant, and shape the Path. –Chip Heath & Dan Heath[5]

_____

_____

_____

---

5. Chip Heath and Dan Heath, *Switch: How to Change Things When Change Is Hard* (New York: Broadway Books, 2010).

124

Big change is rarely accomplished with big solutions. It's instead most often solved by a sequence of small solutions, over months or years.

_____

_____

_____

125

Clarity dissolves resistance. Set a compelling destination—marry the long-term goal with short-term moves, build habits, and rally the herd.

_____

_____

_____

126

Motivate follow-up: after training, make people feel as though they're already closer to the finish line than they might have thought.

_____

_____

_____

127

Small targets lead to small victories, and small victories can often trigger a positive spiral of behavior.

_____

_____

_____

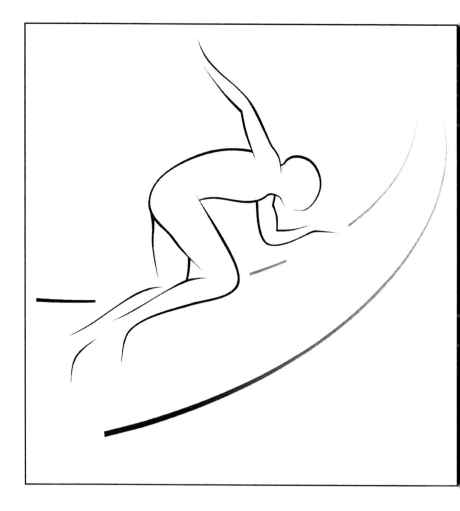

Section VI

Getting Started

What will it take to make the model work for
yourself and how do you get started?

128

Practice helps learners test ideas and decide that change is possible.

_____

_____

_____

129

Shrink the change. Instead of focusing on what's new and different about the change to come, remind people what's already been conquered.

_____

_____

_____

130

Ask learners to apply what they learned for five minutes a day for a week. Make the change small enough that they can't help but succeed.

131

Walk learners a few steps down the path by having them figure out how they will use the training to address their own specific challenges.

132

Set up a list of specific behaviors with direct reports, and meet weekly to discuss what is working, and to provide support and direction.

_____

_____

_____

133

Suggest that learners set up digital reminders (e.g., on their e-mail or mobile calendars) to apply what they have learned.

_____

_____

_____

134

When you engineer early successes, you're engineering hope. Once learners begin to make progress, it's important to make it visible.

_____

_____

_____

135

Draw on social influence to motivate
and support learners—cohort praise,
acceptance, and approval of fellow learners
and peers.

_____

_____

_____

136

Encourage learners to share plans
with others. They're far more likely to
follow through than if they just make
commitments to themselves.

_____

_____

_____

137

Have learners pick one behavior that they can improve on over time, set a goal, practice it, reflect on their progress, and set a new goal.

_____

_____

_____

138

Remind learners that mornings are the best time to start a new habit.

_____

_____

_____

139

Share victories and struggles with one another. Those with early successes can mentor others and get the herd moving.

_____

_____

_____

140

Encourage learners to set small goals
for applying what they recently learned,
or what they plan to learn. Tiny successes
snowball.

_____

_____

_____

What Are Your Ahas?

Thank you for reading *#SUCCESSFUL CORPORATE LEARNING tweet Book10*! Got any "ahas" that would fit with this book?

We'd love to read them! Please send us your ahas by visiting the following URL:

http://tinyurl.com/whatareyourahas

About the Authors

John Moxley, PhD, is the director of leadership development at Cricket Communications. Graduating with high honors from the University of Michigan, John is a learning and talent management expert with 25+ years of experience across industries. He obtained two graduate degrees from Indiana University, and spent 10 years as a media producer before focusing on learning technology.

John's award-winning work includes 75+ custom solutions and over one hundred commercial training titles. Responsible for Cricket University, today he is pioneering ways to integrate mLearning, gamification, and behavioral reinforcement techniques to dramatically improve people performance and achieve Cricket's business goals.

Mitchell Levy, CEO, thought leader architect and CEO of THiNKaha®, has successfully founded over 15 firms and partnerships, is a well-known business consultant, strategist, and educator and an Amazon bestselling author with 18 business books. Mr. Levy is a frequent media guest and a popular speaker, lecturing on business and management issues throughout the United States and around the world. Mr. Levy has provided strategic consulting to over one hundred companies, has advised over five hundred CEOs on critical business issues through the CEO networking groups he's run, and has been Chairman of the Board of a NASDAQ-listed company.

Today, Mr. Levy's principal focus is turning corporate leaders and experts into recognized thought leaders in their spaces. He does this through speeches, coaching, mentoring, various tools and partnerships, and his highly successful physical and eBook publishing businesses where he's published over 225 titles.

Mr. Levy is also executive director of College Open Textbooks/Open Doors Group which works to evangelize the use of open textbooks at four-year institutions and community colleges. Previously, Mr. Levy spent 13 years working for corporations in IT, finance, and operations, including Sun Microsystems where he ran the e-commerce component of Sun's supply chain. He has created four executive education programs at two different Silicon Valley Universities, was the conference chair for four Comdex conferences focusing on business executives at medium-to-large sized enterprises, has contributed to and written over one hundred articles, given over 250 speeches on e-commerce and business, and has prognosticated and published an annual top ten business trends for over a decade at the turn of the century. Mr. Levy earned a BS in operations research from the University of Miami and an MBA from the College of William and Mary.

Books in the THiNKaha® Series

The THiNKaha book series is for thinking adults who lack the time or desire to read long books, but want to improve themselves with knowledge of the most up-to-date subjects. THiNKaha is a leader in timely, cutting-edge books and mobile applications from relevant experts that provide valuable information in a fun, Twitter-brief format for a fast-paced world.

They are available online at http://thinkaha.com or at other online and physical bookstores.

CPSIA information can be obtained at www.ICGtesting.com
Printed in the USA
LVOW12s1623021113

359726LV00001B/9/P